Birds

Ploffskin, Pluffskin, Pelican jee!
We think no birds so happy as we!
Plumpkin, Ploshkin, Pelican jill!
We think so then, and we thought so still!

Edward Lear

The eagle

He clasps the crag with hookèd hands:
Close to the sun in lonely lands,
Ringed with the azure world, he stands.

The wrinkled sea beneath him crawls;
He watches from his mountain walls.
And like a thunderbolt he falls.

Alfred, Lord Tennyson

 two

Grey goose and gander,
Waft your wings together.
Carry the good king's daughter
Over the one-strand river.

three

I saw eight magpies in a tree,
Two for you and six for me:

One for sorrow,

two for mirth,

Three for a wedding,

four for a birth:

Five for England,

six for France,

Seven for a fiddler,

eight for a dance.

five

Swan, swan, over the sea
Swim, swan, swim.
Swan, swan, back again
Well swum swan.

Little Trotty Wagtail, he went in the rain,

And twittering, tottering sideways,

he ne'er got straight again;

He stooped to get a worm,

and looked up to get a fly,

And then he flew away

ere his feathers they were dry.

John Clare

There was an Old Man with a beard
Who said, "It is just as I feared! –
Two Owls and a Hen, four Larks and a Wren,
Have all built their nests in my beard!"

Edward Lear

Three little Tom-tits
All lost their wits
When first they saw
A pig in fits.

Little Robin Redbreast sat upon a rail;
Niddle naddle went his head,
Wiggle waggle went his tail.

Little Rob Robin,
Where do you live?
Up in yonder wood, sir,
On a hazel twig.

The cock is crowing,
The stream is flowing,
The small birds twitter,
The lake doth glitter,
The green field sleeps in the sun.

The oldest and youngest
Are at work with the strongest:
The cattle are grazing,
Their heads never raising,
There are forty feeding like one!

William Wordsworth

eleven

Riddle me, riddle me ree
A hawk sat up in a tree;
And he said to himself said he,
"Oh dear! what a fine bird I be."

twelve

The dove says, "Coo
What shall I do?
It's hard, it's hard to keep my two."

"Pooh", says the wren,
"Why, I've got ten
And keep them all like gentlemen."

thirteen

Toucannery

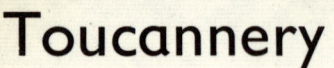

whatever one toucan can do
is sooner done by toucans two
and three toucans it's very true
can do much more than two can do

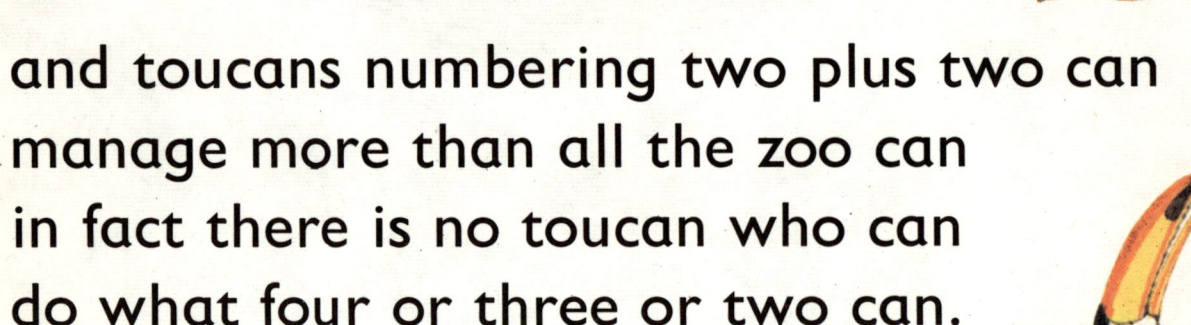

and toucans numbering two plus two can
manage more than all the zoo can
in fact there is no toucan who can
do what four or three or two can.

                    Jack Prelutsky

The Dodo used to walk around
And take the sun and air,
The Sun yet warms his native ground –
The Dodo is not there!
That voice which used to squawk and squeak
Is now forever dumb –
Yet may you see his bones and beak
All in the Museum.

Hilaire Belloc

fifteen

Go to bed first –
A golden purse.

Go to bed second –
A golden pheasant.

Go to bed third –
A golden bird.

sixteen